Bible Story
Skits Kids Can Do

24 Quick and Easy Scripts
for Ages 8 to 12

STANDARD PUBLISHING

Cincinnati, Ohio

Bible Story Skits Kids Can Do

Standard Publishing, Cincinnati, Ohio
A division of Standex International Corporation
© 1999 Standard Publishing
All rights reserved
Printed in the United States of America

Cover and inside design: Diana Walters
Graphic layout: Dale Meyers
Editor: Heather Turner
Acquisitions editors: Lise Caldwell, Ruth Frederick

06 05 04 03 02 01 00 99   5 4 3 2 1

ISBN: 0-7847-1074-0

Contents

Introduction

Bible Story Skits Kids Can Do is an easy-to-use children's ministry resource designed to help teach children important Bible stories. Each skit takes minimal planning and rehearsal, and many skits involve your entire group. The following are tips on how to use the audience participation activities with groups of various sizes, as well as rehearsal tips and simple memorization pointers.

Usage Guide for Large and Small Groups

These skits can be used by groups of 20 or 200! We want to help you adapt these skits to fit your own situation. Each skit has a section called Scene Setup. As you read through Scene Setup, here are some directions for specific circumstances.

Groups of 25 or Fewer

Often there is a role for all/some of your children. You will use all your children in these parts. Direction given for positioning the characters refer to the performance area. You will use the room itself as the performance area.

Often there is no audience, and the action of the drama will take place right in the middle of all the children. Any suggestions for audience participation will be performed by all the children.

Groups of More Than 25

Often there is a role for all/some of your children. You will use some of your children.

Directions given for positioning the characters refer to the performance area. If you do not have an actual stage, you will designate a portion of your room to be the performance area, with the remaining children forming the audience.

There may be suggestions for audience participation. For example, the audience may be asked to join some of the children on the stage in chanting a refrain or making specific sound effects. Consider each script to determine whether or not it is practical for all the children to join in.

Also stay alert for roles that can be divided and assigned to more than one child. For instance, you may use two or three narrators instead of only one. This not only involves more children in active participation, but also reduces the amount of memorization required by any one child. And remember, many roles can be either male or female with a simple change of a name!

Rehearsal and Memorization Tips

Involve as many interested children as you can as primary actors. While a few roles may call for a strong, charismatic actor, most of them do not. Encourage children who are reluctant to give acting a try, but never force an unwilling child to get on stage.

Give your actors the script a week or two in advance, if possible. Have them read it out loud. Explain any words or concepts with which they are unfamiliar. It is difficult to memorize something you don't understand! Provide highlighters for each actor to highlight her part.

Read the Scripture verse or passage out loud. Consider giving a brief lesson or devotional on the topic. Ask your actors if they identify with the story or struggle. How?

Now have the actors read the script aloud again. This time have them act out the scene. Tell them when to stand, sit, walk, enter, and exit. Encourage them to write these instructions on their photocopy of the script. If anyone seems to be struggling with meaning or pronunciation, clarify it for him.

Instruct your actors to look at their scripts every day. They should

• Read the script several times straight through, then try to summarize the story line in their own words.

• Read it through again, this time covering their own lines, trying to remember them as they go.

• Once they are able to do this, have them ask someone to read the lines out loud with them, allowing the actors to recite their own lines.

If a child finds memorization difficult, but wants to act, encourage him to record the entire script on a tape and listen to it frequently. Then he can record himself reading all the lines but his, leaving pauses for him to say his lines.

You will need one more rehearsal, which can be just before the performance, or at a separate time. Begin this rehearsal with a few silly tongue twisters or a goofy game, in the performance area if possible. This will help the children relax and begin to behave naturally in the performance space.

Then have them rehearse the scene. Encourage them to be relaxed, have fun, and speak naturally (and loudly). Emphasize that they should speak each word clearly and distinctly. Correct any blocking (stage movement) they may have missed or forgotten.

Before you perform, gather your actors and pray with them. Pray that they will remember their lines, remain calm, and help their peers understand the lesson. After the performance, remember to give positive feedback, especially to insecure or inexperienced actors.

Scripture
Genesis 1

Props
flashlights (as many as possible)
a hula hoop wrapped in tinfoil

Characters
Shawn
Lennie

Scene Setup
Turn off the lights to darken the room. Distribute flashlights and ask children to practice turning them on at your signal. Ask children to put down their flashlights (which will become a distraction otherwise).

Say, "There will come a point in our skit when it's time to turn on the flashlights. I'll signal you when that time comes by counting 1 . . . 2 . . . 3 . . . flash! When I say that, shine your lights in the eyes of our actors, but stay quiet so you can hear the rest of the skit."

Script

Shawn *and* Lennie *walk onto stage and take turns stepping through the hula hoop. As each actor passes through the hoop, he acts as if he's floating.*

Shawn: Wow! It worked! Lennie, your time-travel hoop worked!

Lennie: At last! Success! This year at the Science Fair, Melissa's "Molds of North America" display is toast!

Shawn: But where are we? We're just sort of floating in the middle of . . . nothing.

Lennie: Not possible. You've always got to be somewhere.

Shawn: Maybe we traveled back before the beginning of time.

Lennie: No way! There must just be . . . wait! Did you hear that?

Shawn: It sounded like a voice.

Signal children to turn on their flashlights. Shawn *and* Lennie *blink as if blinded by an intense light.*

Lennie: Hey! Turn off the headlights!

Shawn: Those aren't headlights—but it's some kind of light. Listen . . . the voice again . . . now there's water . . . and dry land . . . it's the earth! This must be the creation of the earth—and we're in the very first morning!

Lennie: Then that means the voice we heard . . .

Shawn: Right. It's God speaking everything into existence. If we stay here long enough we'll see God create plants, and the sun and moon, and the seas and the dry land.

Lennie: How long until he creates food?

Shawn: Umm . . . that's on day six, I think.

Lennie: Then let's go home. I want lunch and I'm not waiting six days!

Shawn *and* Lennie *pass through the hula hoop and exit*

Digging Deeper

ᔓ   When you consider that God created everything by speaking, how do you feel about God's power?

ᔓ   If you had been present for creation, what would you most like to have seen God create?

ᔓ   Where do you see God's creative power in the world now?

Scripture
Genesis 6–9

Props
two pieces of wood
two hammers

Characters
Noah
Shem

Scene Setup
Tell children who aren't acting that they will provide animal sound effects. When they hear the name of an animal, they should provide five seconds of sound effects. Children are not to act like animals, just provide sound effects.

Have children rehearse making horse, tiger, and snake sound effects.

——— Script ———

Noah *is hammering a piece of wood with a hammer when* Shem *enters.* Shem *carries a length of two by four wood and* Noah *pauses.*

Noah: We're almost finished with the ark, son. How's the gopher wood supply?

Shem: Dad, we've cut down every gopher tree inside ten miles to build this thing. This piece came out of my bed. Why can't we just use another kind of wood?

Noah: The Lord said to use gopher wood, Shem. So gopher wood it is.

Shem: Dad, all I do is go-fer wood. Then I go-fer animal food to store down below deck. Then I go-fer this and go-fer that . . . I'm tired of it!

Noah: Be patient, son.

Shem: I've been patient, Dad! We've been working on this ark for almost a hundred years! A hundred years! All to get ready for a flood that never came!

Noah: The Lord keeps his promises, Shem.

Shem: Starting when? Look, Dad, every other kid in the neighborhood grew up to be a farmer, or shepherd, or shopkeeper. All I know how to do is build arks. How am I supposed to make a living? We live miles from the ocean—nobody around here wants an ark!

Noah: When the flood comes, you'll be glad you believed God's promises, Shem.

Shem: Don't you get it, Dad? God forgot about his promise! It's been a hundred years!

Noah: The Lord never forgets.

Shem: "Never forgets his promises," right. If you've said that once, you've said it a thousand times. But Dad, look down there. [*pulls Noah to edge of stage and looks at audience*]

Noah: Lots of animals.

Indicate to the children that they should make their animal sound effects now

Shem: It's a zoo! We've got snakes down there. Dogs. Parrots. Seals. Monkeys. Cows. Horses. Lions. Tigers. Bears. We've even got termites. You're bringing termites on a wooden ark?

Noah: Just two.

Shem: Dad, when will you get it through your head? God has forgotten his promise!

Noah: [*looks up*] See those dark clouds?

Shem: [*looks up*] It does look like rain. After all this time. [Shem *grabs other hammer and starts to pound on wood*] What are you waiting for, Dad? We've got an ark to finish!

Noah *smiles and joins* Shem *in hammering*

Digging Deeper

෪ How do you feel when someone breaks a promise to you?

෪ What's the longest you can remember waiting for someone to keep a promise?

෪ What's a promise God made to you that he hasn't kept yet? Will he keep it? If you answered "yes," why do you think so? If you answered "no," why do you think God won't keep the promise he's made to you?

Scripture
Exodus 16, 17

Props
"manna" (individually wrapped snack crackers or boxes of raisins)

Characters
Moses
Larry

Scene Setup
Have all/some children play the part of the Jews who are on the Exodus with *Moses*. Their role is to grumble and to grumble with sincerity. Tell them they'll know when to grumble; it's written into the script.

    You have a special role. You'll distribute "manna" when the time is appropriate. Be sure to hide the snacks from view until the time arrives to toss them to the audience. If possible, stand behind the seated children so the "manna" falls from the sky as a total surprise.

Script

Moses is standing on stage when Larry walks up to him

Larry: Moses, I'm sorry to interrupt, but can I talk with you?

Moses: Certainly.

Larry: Moses, the people were wondering if there's a drive-thru window anywhere up ahead.

Moses: A drive-thru window? What for?

Larry: Well, everyone is hungry. Nobody's eaten a decent meal since we left Egypt. Their stomachs are grumbling.

Pause for audience's grumbling reaction

Moses: But we have at least a half-million people here. The multitude stretches as far as the eye can see!

Larry: Which means the line at the drive-thru window may be long. But at least we'll get lunch.

Moses: There's no drive-thru window up ahead.

Larry: Grocery store?

Moses: No grocery store.

Larry: Pizza delivery?

Moses: There's no food of any sort. We're crossing a great wilderness, remember?

Larry: Then why did you bring us out here? At least back in Egypt we had enough to eat and drink. And at night I could sleep. Out here the tummy-grumbling keeps me awake all night.

Pause for audience reaction

Moses: Don't worry—the Lord has said there will be food. It will rain down bread from heaven.

Larry: Bread from heaven? You're kidding, right?

Moses: Not at all. Look! [*points to sky*] Here comes something to eat now!

Toss the snacks so they fall among the children, who will delightedly scoop them up. Reserve some to give to children who don't manage to grab an equal share.

Moses: Are you feeling better now?

Larry: Absolutely! God takes good care of his people!

Digging Deeper

2 Name a way God has taken care of you or your family.

2 Name some needs you have. Name some wants you have. Which does God promise to provide?

Last One There Gets the Lobby

Scripture
Luke 2:1-11

Props
none

Characters
Man
Woman
Child
Innkeeper

Scene Setup
Have some/all of the children play the part of visitors in Bethlehem who have already rented rooms for the night. Position your three travelers so they're standing facing the audience. Position the *Innkeeper* so he or she is to one side of your performance area.

Say, "You are the fortunate ones who have found a hotel room. You've unpacked, pulled off your sandals, and now you're stretched out on the bed, relaxing after your long journey. When asked if you want to give up your rooms, your response is 'No way!'"

Ask children to practice their response several times. Explain that they will know when to deliver their line.

Script

The three travelers are positioned so that Child *is in the middle and slightly behind* Man *and* Woman. *The three are walking in place.*

Child: Are we there yet?

Man: No! And if I've told you once, I've told you a hundred times: we aren't in Bethlehem yet!

Child: But I've got to go!

Woman: [*whining*] Why didn't Caesar Augustus count us where we live? Why did we have to come all the way to Bethlehem?

Child: I'm hungry.

Man: Those are the rules. I don't make the rules, I just obey them. Especially Caesar's rules.

Woman: At last—Bethlehem! I hope we can find a place to stay.

Child: I'm hungry and I have to go!

Man: Well, we'd better try here before we get too far into town.

The three travelers walk up to Innkeeper

Man: Excuse me, Sir. Do you have a room for three to rent?

Innkeeper: Nope. Full up, just like every other hotel in town. Of course, someone who's already here might want to give up a room. Hey—anyone here want to give up a room?

Indicate to the audience that it is time to shout "No Way!"

Innkeeper: Sorry. Of course, I could rent you this room.

Woman: But this is the lobby!

Innkeeper: It's got a roof and a floor. And it's the last room in town. Take it or leave it.

Child: Come on, Dad!

Man: We'll take it. Four nights.

Innkeeper: Good choice. I'll go get you a blanket. [*exits*]

Woman: We can't stay here!

Man: You heard him. This is the last room in town. And you don't want to be like that couple out there, do you? [*points as if out a window*]

Woman: Those poor people. The woman is about to have a baby and that man looks so tired.

Man: Don't worry about them. They'll find a place to stay. Someone will feel sorry for them.

Woman: I hope so.

Child: Hey! I still have to go and I mean now!

Man: Come on. Let's all go find the outhouse.

All exit

Digging Deeper

∿ If people had known Jesus was the Messiah, do you think they'd have found room for Mary and Joseph?

∿ If you'd had a room in an inn, would you have given it up for Joseph and Mary? Why or why not?

∿ Are you making room for Jesus in your heart? In what ways?

Seeing by Believing

Scripture
Mark 10:45-52

Props
none

Characters
Bartimaeus
Jesus
Peter
Narrator

Scene Setup
Have some/all children play the part of a crowd listening to *Jesus*. Explain that the crowd's role is to react when *Jesus* heals *Bartimaeus*. If you have fewer than 25 children, this can be a performance "in the round" with the crowd surrounding the actors in this play. Place the crowd in a semicircle behind the characters for larger groups.

   This is a silent production. No one but the designated reader will actually say anything. Tell children they're to silently act out their roles. Ask a strong reader to read the following script, pausing where indicated so the actors can act out their roles.

——————— Script ———————

Bartimaeus *is seated on the floor.* Jesus *and* Peter *are surrounded by a crowd that's listening to* Jesus *speak.*

Narrator: When Jesus, his disciples, and a large crowd were leaving the city of Jericho, a blind man named Bartimaeus was sitting by the side of the road, begging.

Narrator *pauses to allow actors to portray the spoken words*

Narrator: When he heard that Jesus was in the crowd passing by he shouted, "Jesus, Son of David, have mercy on me!"

Narrator *pauses to allow actors to portray the spoken words*

Narrator: Many of the people in the crowd told the beggar to be quiet.

Narrator *pauses to allow actors to portray the spoken words*

Narrator: But Bartimaeus just shouted louder: "Jesus, Son of David, have mercy on me!"

Narrator *pauses to allow actors to portray the spoken words*

Narrator: Jesus stopped and said, "Call him."

Narrator *pauses to allow actors to portray the spoken words*

Narrator: The people called to the blind beggar, "Cheer up. He's calling for you."

Narrator *pauses to allow actors to portray the spoken words*

Narrator: So Bartimaeus rose to his feet, [*pause*] cast his cloak aside, [*pause*] and made his way to Jesus [*pause*]. "What do you want me to do for you?" asked Jesus. [*pause*] The blind man answered, "Rabbi, I want to see." [*pause*] Jesus said, "Go. Your faith has healed you." [*pause*] Immediately Bartimaeus could see. [*pause*] He was so excited, [*pause*] and so were the people who saw this miracle. [*pause*] The beggar didn't go back to beg any more. He followed Jesus along the road.

Digging Deeper

꒰ Why do you think Jesus could instantly heal people?

꒰ If you'd seen Jesus perform this miracle, how would you have described it to people who weren't there? Do you think they would have believed you? Why or why not?

꒰ If you could have been present to see a miracle of Jesus, which one would you most like to have seen? Why?

Scripture
Luke 19:1-10

Props
stepladder
baseball

Characters
Zacchaeus
Fan One
Fan Two
Fan Three

Scene Setup
Have some/all of the children be unhappy taxpayers.

Say, "You know you've been cheated by having to pay too many taxes—and it's Zacchaeus who has cheated you. You don't like Zacchaeus, and if you get a chance you'll say so." Have children practice delivering a resounding chorus of "boo's" and raspberries at your command. Tell children to watch for their invitation to call out their displeasure with Zacchaeus.

Note: It helps to cast an actor for the role of *Zacchaeus* who is slightly shorter than the three fans—but not essential. If *Zacchaeus* is taller than the three, just ask *Zacchaeus* to lean over to appear shorter.

Script

Zacchaeus *is offstage.* Fan one, Fan two, *and* Fan Three *stand in a row, shoulder to shoulder, facing the audience. They peer to their left, craning their necks, attempting to be first to see the approaching Jesus. The stepladder is behind them.*

Fan One: Is he coming yet? I don't see him.

Fan Two: Are you sure he's coming this way?

Fan One: If he's coming out of Jericho, Jesus will pass by here. And I'm going to see him. Did you know he can turn water into wine?

Fan Three: I heard he can make lame people walk and blind people see.

Fan Two: [*pulls out baseball*] I just want him to autograph this ball.

Zacchaeus *walks behind three* Fans. *He stands on his tiptoes and still can't see over them.*

Zacchaeus: Excuse me, I need to stand in front of you.

Fan One: Forget it! We've been standing here for hours so we can see Jesus.

Zacchaeus: Perhaps you don't know who I am. I'm a very important person.

Fan One: We know exactly who you are. You're Zacchaeus, and you've been cheating us out of extra taxes for years. Get lost.

Zacchaeus: You'd better be nice to me. I have a lot of friends.

Fan Three: Really? Anyone here a friend of Zacchaeus?

Indicate to audience to deliver boo's and catcalls

Zacchaeus: But I can't see. I'm too short to see over the crowd!

Fan One: Then climb that tree and hang up there with the rest of the nuts.

Fan Two: Hey! He's coming! I can see him coming!

Zacchaeus climbs up the stepladder so he can see, then peers left along with the rest

Fan Three: Boy, the nerve of that guy!

Fan One: Yeah. Like Jesus would even talk to a tax collector like that anyway!

Fan Three: With any luck he'll fall out of the tree and break his neck.

Fan Two: [*calling*] Jesus! Will you autograph this ball?

Digging Deeper

- Jesus talked with Zacchaeus. Why do you think Jesus did that?

- People didn't like Zacchaeus much. How did Jesus show he loved Zacchaeus?

- If Jesus told you he was coming to your house for lunch, how would that feel? How do you think Zacchaeus felt? Why?

Scripture
Luke 3:2-14

Props
microphone (a pencil held eraser-up will work)
videocassette recorder and video tape (optional)

Characters
Reporter
Person One
Person Two

Scene Setup
Have some/all of the children be John the Baptist's audience. They can huddle around to watch the interview, just like people do during television on-the-street interviews. Encourage the *Reporter* to hold the microphone up as if speaking into it and to hold it up to the people being interviewed.

Consider using a videocassette recorder to tape the interview. Then show the tape to reinforce what was said.

Say, "Here you are at the Jordan River. You've just heard John the Baptist speak, and now a television crew is on hand to interview some of you."

Script

Reporter *stands in center of the performing area. The two people being interviewed flank the* Reporter. *The rest of the children stand around listening.*

Reporter: This is Jack (Jane) Jackson, live at the Jordan River. It's nothing short of a spectacle here in this rugged wilderness setting. Hundreds of people have walked here from neighboring towns to hear John the Baptist speak. I have two members of John's audience here with me now. [*to* Person One] Sir, what is it about John that's so unusual?

Person One: He wears camel hair clothes and eats honey and locusts. That's pretty unusual.

Reporter: True. But what did John say today?

Person One: He said you're a sinner.

Reporter: He said what?!

Person One: Well, he said we're all sinners. I guess that includes you.

Person Two: John says we all need to be forgiven by God. That we've all done things that don't please God. And we should ask God to forgive us and change our hearts and minds.

Reporter: Let me see if I have this right. John tells people that they've done bad things.

Person One: Right.

Reporter: And people walk all the way out here knowing he'll say things like that?

Person Two: Right again. John always says the same thing: People need to ask God for forgiveness and to change how they live.

Reporter: Doesn't that message make people angry? I noticed there are a lot of religious leaders in the crowd today. They must get upset when John tells them they have to change how they live to please God.

Person One: People never like to hear that they've sinned, but what John says is true. We're all sinners and we all need to be forgiven by God. Even you.

Person Two: Right.

Reporter: That's the story here at the Jordan River. A story of preaching forgiveness and repenting. Now back to you, Ted.

Digging Deeper

- If John the Baptist was preaching repentance and forgiveness today, do you think anyone would come hear him talk? Why or why not?

- Have you asked God to forgive you for your sins? How did that feel?

An Eye-Opening Experience

Scripture
Luke 24:13-35

Props
loaf of uncut bread
small table

Characters
Cleopas
Judy
Jesus

Scene Setup
Gather some/all of your children in a semicircle around the performance area. Place *Cleopas* and *Judy* in the center of the performance area, facing the audience. Tell them to march in place as they talk, as though they're walking the dusty road to Emmaus.

Ask *Jesus* to join them at the appropriate time. Place the bread on a table to one side of the performance area.

———— Script ————

Cleopas *and* Judy *walk in place as they talk*

Cleopas: What I don't understand is how Jesus' body could just disappear. The Romans don't have it.

Judy: And the Jewish leaders must not have it or they'd have shown it to the world.

Cleopas: And we don't have it. Yet, it's gone. That giant stone was rolled away and Jesus' body was gone. It's a mystery.

Judy: It's so sad. I was hoping that Jesus really was the Messiah, God's chosen one.

Cleopas: You and me both.

Jesus *enters*

Jesus: You two must be walking to Emmaus.

Cleopas: That's right, stranger. You're welcome to join us.

Jesus: What were you talking about?

Cleopas: You don't know? You must be the only one in Jerusalem who didn't hear about Jesus being killed.

Judy: He was a prophet, powerful in word and deed before God and the people. But the chief priests and our rulers handed him over to be crucified. That was three days ago.

Cleopas: And this morning some of our friends went to the tomb and didn't find his body. They said an angel told them Jesus was alive.

Jesus: You're so slow to believe the things that the prophets told you. Didn't the Messiah have to suffer and then enter his glory? Listen while we walk. I'll explain to you what the Scriptures say about the Christ.

They walk in place silently for a few seconds, waving their arms as if talking, then they stop to speak

Judy: Well, here we are. Home sweet home.

Cleopas: [*to* Jesus] Say, why don't you stay the night at our house? It's getting dark.

Jesus: No, I really must keep going.

Cleopas: I insist. It's the least we can do after all the teaching you've given to us. Come in and eat.

They walk over to the table

Judy: In fact, you break the bread for us. We'd be honored.

Jesus: [*bowing in prayer*] Thank you, Father, for this bread and for these two people who want to serve you. Open their eyes, Lord.

Cleopas: Thank you. I—wait! I know you!

Judy: You're him! You're Jesus!

Cleopas: And you're alive!

Jesus *smiles and quickly walks off stage as* Cleopas *and* Judy *stand in amazement*

Judy: Can you believe it? Jesus in the flesh!

Cleopas: Come on—we've got to go tell the others back in Jerusalem. Right now!

Cleopas *and* Judy *dash off stage*

(Pick up the bread and lead children in prayer. Ask God to open our eyes to Jesus, for every one who shares the bread to understand Jesus is alive. Then pass out the bread.)

Digging Deeper

- How do you think the two people who walked with Jesus felt when they realized he was alive and eating with them? Why?

- If you'd been the people who walked with Jesus, do you think you'd have recognized him? Why or why not?

- What difference does it make in your life that Jesus is alive?

Knee-Deep in Sheep

Scripture
Psalm 23

Props
inexpensive acoustic guitar or other stringed instrument
chair

Characters
Narrator
David

Scene Setup
Seat *David* on a chair and give him a guitar to strum. Instruct some/all of the children to sit on the floor near *David*. Tell the "sheep" to get on their hands and knees and practice saying "baa." When you think they've got their line down, begin the skit, pausing as indicated for the actors to take the appropriate action.

Say, "Any passerby would assume this is about to be a sing-along. That passerby would be wrong. What we have here is a shepherd who's writing a song. And the shepherd is, you could say, knee-deep in sheep.

Script

David *sits on the chair with the guitar on his lap, strumming to the sheep, who are milling around*

Narrator: David was a shepherd when he was a young man. He'd sit on a rock and as his sheep grazed contentedly, he'd write beautiful songs to the Lord.

David *dreamily strums his guitar*

Narrator: Being a shepherd, David understood how God's people needed a good shepherd. Often, David had to put down his musical instrument to tend to his sheep.

David *puts down his guitar and pats a few "sheep" on the head*

Narrator: David would tell his sheep to lie down and rest in green pastures.

David *gestures for sheep to lie down*

Narrator: David helped his sheep find still water to drink.

David *pretends to splash water on his sheep*

Narrator: He guided his sheep on safe paths.

David *leads several of his sheep down a "path"*

Narrator: And because there were many sheep-eating enemies about, David protected his sheep.

David *mimes fighting off a bear*

Narrator: David's flock couldn't have found a more caring shepherd.

David *"herds" his sheep together*

Narrator: David's sheep would follow him anywhere.

David *leads the sheep down a "path"*

Narrator: Anywhere, that is, except home for lunch when he was planning to eat lamb chops.

Sheep scamper off in all directions

Digging Deeper

- In what ways has God been a good shepherd by taking care of you?

- In what ways has God been a good shepherd by providing for you?

- In what ways has God been a good shepherd by guiding you?

Scripture
Genesis 37–41

Props
chair
stack of files or other papers

Characters
Royal Interviewer
Joseph

Scene Setup
Seat the *Royal Interviewer* on a chair facing the audience. Give this person a stack of papers as if he's been evaluating many job applications.

Script

The Royal Interviewer *is tired, weary, and a bit impatient as the last appointment is called in*

Royal Interviewer: There are days I hate this job. The Pharaoh decides he needs a second-in-command and suddenly I have to interview everybody who wants the job—which is half the country! Why couldn't I have just been a chariot driver like my mother wanted? [*calling*] Next!

Joseph *enters*

Joseph: Good afternoon.

Royal Interviewer: Yeah. Whatever. Now let's get down to business. So your name is Joseph and you want to run Egypt.

Joseph: Actually, Pharaoh already asked me to take the job.

Royal Interviewer: [*sarcastically*] Sure he did. And I can jump over the pyramids. Now let's just go through this form, shall we? What's your background?

Joseph: Well, I was a shepherd until my brothers sold me into slavery.

Royal Interviewer: You were a shepherd? Then a slave?

Joseph:	Right. And here in Egypt I ran a family's household until I was thrown into prison.
Royal Interviewer:	Prison. [*sarcastically*] This just keeps getting better and better.
Joseph:	But while I was in prison, Pharaoh had a dream. I was the only one who could tell him what it meant. So now I'm going to be in charge of the entire country.
Royal Interviewer:	Let's review. Shepherd, slave, prisoner, and reader of dreams. Does that sound like someone who gets to run Egypt? I don't think so.
Joseph:	But Pharaoh already gave me the job.
Royal Interviewer:	And he forgot to tell me, right? So I've been wasting my time interviewing the last 375 people who want the job? Fat chance, buddy. Look, it's been a long day. I'll forget you played this little joke if you walk out of here this minute. Otherwise, I'll call a guard and you'll be in the Nile wrestling crocodiles before you know what hit you.
Joseph:	I'll leave, but listen. I'm the new ruler. You're working for me now.
Royal Interviewer:	Don't make it worse than it already is, buddy. You see that room full of people there? [*indicate audience*] Any one of them could do a better job than you running Egypt. Now get outta here!

Joseph *leaves, then* Royal Interviewer *stands to leave*

Royal Interviewer:	[*to audience*] All of you people waiting to apply for the job, forget it. I'm going home to see what's for supper. And I'm going to try and forget that nut who was just in here. A foreign slave being the ruler of Egypt? It would take an act of God for that to happen.

Royal Interviewer *exits*

Digging Deeper

≳ Would you have picked Joseph to rule Egypt? Why or why not?

≳ Why do you think God picked Joseph for the position?

≳ Do you believe God still picks rulers for nations?

≳ If God picks our country's leader, what does that mean about how we should treat the leader?

From Everlasting to Everlasting

Scripture
Psalm 90:2, 4

Props
music stands (optional)

Characters
Group One, group of three to five children
Group Two, group of three to five children
Group Three, remaining children

Scene Setup
This skit is a Readers Theater, which means your children will read the script aloud together. The script may be projected onto a screen or individual scripts on music stands may be used. Teach the large group the motions for "From everlasting to everlasting you are God" (below).

Explain that the script is actually Scripture drawn from two Psalms and this is more than just a performance. It's a prayer to God, offering him praise and adoration. The script should be delivered with that attitude.

Once your children have mastered this script, consider sharing their reading of it with an adult class, or during the morning worship service.

—— Script ——

Group One: Before the mountains were born, [*children raise their hands over their heads, fingertips touching, making a "mountain" shape*]

Group Two: Or you brought forth the earth and the world, [*children make a circle with their hands, beginning at shoulder height and bringing their hands back together at waist level*]

Group Three: From everlasting to everlasting you are God. [*Children point left with their left hands on the first "everlasting," and right with their right hands on the second "everlasting." On "you are God," children lift both hands in the air.*]

Group One: For a thousand years in your sight, [*children shield their eyes with their right hands*]

Group Two: Are like a day that has just gone by. [*children spin slowly around one time*]

Group One: Or like a watch in the night. [*children march three steps right and then three steps left*]

Group Three: From everlasting to everlasting you are God. [*repeat earlier motions*]

Group Two: Let us praise the name of the Lord, for he commanded and they were created. [*children lift their hands above their heads*]

Group Three: From everlasting to everlasting you are God. [*repeat earlier motions*]

Group One: He set them in place forever and ever. [*children motion as if they are placing stars in the sky by lifting their fists then opening their hands wide*]

Group Three: From everlasting to everlasting you are God. [*repeat earlier motions*]

Group One: He gave a decree that will never pass away. [*children motion as if they are unrolling a parchment*]

Group Three: From everlasting to everlasting you are God. [*repeat earlier motions*]

(Verses adapted from Psalm 90 and 148.)

Digging Deeper

- God was in the beginning and will be there for eternity. How do you feel about this comment?

- The same God who set distant galaxies to spinning knows what you think and feel. How does that make you feel?

- What does it mean to you that the God who loves you is also the Creator?

No Time to Wait

Scripture
John 14:1-3

Props
two chairs placed side by side as if a bench
bag of individually-wrapped candies

Characters
Sarah
James

Scene Setup
Have some/all of the children be a flock of birds that have gathered at the feet of a woman sitting on a park bench. She'll be tossing them "bird feed" (wrapped candy) now and then and they should coo and cluck in appreciation.

Script

Sarah sits in the chair, center stage, facing audience. She looks up, and occasionally to the left and right. Every so often she tosses a few pieces of candy to the birds at her feet. James comes whistling in from stage left, notices her, then pauses to talk.

James: Hi, Sarah.

Sarah: Hi, James.

James: What are you doing?

Sarah: Waiting. And feeding birds.

James: [*looks to the left and right; nothing seems to be happening*] Mind if I sit down?

Sarah: That would be great. Have a seat.

James has a seat and says nothing for 10 seconds. Sarah keeps looking up, and occasionally to the left and right. James joins her. Finally, he can't take the suspense any longer.

James: Sarah, what exactly are you waiting for?

Sarah: I'm waiting for Jesus to come back.

James: Sarah, Jesus is in heaven. The Romans crucified him and he rose from the dead 20 years ago. Remember? I was there in Jerusalem.

Sarah: Right. But he said he'd come back and I don't want to miss it.

James: You know, Jesus didn't say exactly when he'd come back. In fact, he said even he didn't know the exact hour.

Sarah: Fine, but I want to be ready. So I'm waiting.

James: You're just going to sit here feeding birds until Jesus shows up?

Sarah: Yup.

James: Don't you think Jesus would rather you were busy sharing his story with other people while you wait? Or feeding the hungry? Helping the poor? There's a lot of work to do, you know.

Sarah: You don't think he'll be sad if he comes and nobody is waiting?

James: Trust me. I think he'll be just as happy to find everyone doing what he asked them to do.

Sarah: [*rising*] Well, if you think so.

James: I'm sure of it. Come on—there's a lady in town who needs to hear the Good News and you can tell her. I'll introduce you.

Sarah: What about the rest of this bird food?

James: [*takes bag*] This? I guess it's for the birds.

James *tosses rest of candy to the birds,* James *and* Sarah *exit*

Digging Deeper

≳ Do you think James or Sarah was right about what to do until Jesus comes? Should we wait to welcome him or stay busy doing his work until he comes?

≳ If you knew for certain Jesus was returning tomorrow, how would you feel? Why? How would you change what you usually do for the next day?

Giant Trouble

Scripture
1 Samuel 17

Props
marshmallow
yardstick
chopstick or unsharpened pencil for some/all of the children

Characters
Narrator
David
Goliath

Scene Setup
Have some/all of the children be the Israelite army. Give each child a chopstick or an unsharpened pencil. Give *David* a marshmallow and a reminder not to eat it! Give *Goliath* a yardstick. Tell the children to act out the narration—but the Israelite army cannot stand or move from their line. Before beginning, take aside the child playing the role of *Goliath* and explain that he can stand when he's introduced and stay standing. He should be as threatening as possible without actually touching or harming anyone.

Say, "Here we have the mighty Israelite army, camped on low hills on one side of a valley. They are heavily armed and prepared for battle. They're just waiting for the signal to attack the army on the other side of the valley."

Script

David *and the rest of the children sit on the floor, cross-legged, in a line facing* Goliath

Narrator: The Israelite army was gathered for war. They'd pitched their tents on the low hills rimming one side of a valley. On the other side of the valley waited the Philistine army.

The Israelites were certain of victory. They raised their spears and shouted boldly. [*pause*] They punched each other in the shoulders and told jokes, [*pause*] always keeping an eye on the Philistines. [*pause*] The Israelite soldiers nodded in agreement: The Philistines were toast. [*pause*]

Until Goliath walked down into the valley. [*pause*]

Goliath was huge. He was bigger than huge, standing nine feet tall and towering over the Israelites. [*pause*] He carried a tremendous, iron-tipped spear. [*pause*] And he growled out taunts to the Israelites. [*pause*]

Goliath: Why do you come out and line up for battle? Choose a man and have him come down to me. If he is able to fight and kill me, we will become your subjects. If I kill him, you will serve us. I dare you!

Narrator: Goliath came out to make fun of the Israelites every morning and night for 40 days. [*pause*] The Israelites felt ashamed. They hid their faces. [*pause*] They put down their spears. [*pause*] There was no more proud shouting.

Then David came forward. [*pause*] David was small, but he convinced King Saul to send him to fight Goliath. David took no sword or shield, just a sling and 5 smooth stones. [*pause*] When David entered the valley Goliath said,

Goliath: Come here and I'll give your flesh to the birds of the air and the beasts of the field!

Narrator: David answered,

David: You come against me with sword and javelin, but I come against you in the name of the Lord Almighty, the God of the armies of Israel. This day the Lord will hand you over to me. All those gathered here will know that it is not by sword or spear that the Lord saves. For the battle is the Lord's, and he will give all of you into our hands.

Narrator: Goliath roared in anger. [*pause*] He prepared his mighty spear to throw at David. [*pause*] But David rushed at Goliath and with his sling threw one smooth stone that hit Goliath in the head. [*pause while* David *throws his marshmallow at* Goliath] The giant toppled. [*pause*] Then David drew Goliath's sword and killed the giant. [*pause*] The Israelites shouted in victory and joy. [*pause*] The battle was won!

Digging Deeper

2 Do you think David was afraid? Why or why not? How would you have felt?

2 God helped David face a challenge. What challenges has God helped you face?

Against All Odds

Scripture
1 Kings 18

Props
book of matches
pencil baton

Characters
Coach
Elijah

Scene Setup
Have some/all of the children play the part of a bloodthirsty crowd screaming for a fight. Explain that even a bloodthirsty crowd needs to be directed, and position yourself as if you were a choir director, facing your shouters. Ask them to demand a fight on your command, and to raise the volume as you're raising your pencil baton. Raise and lower the volume several times and when they're taking direction well, launch into a 30-second practice session.

   Position *Elijah* in a chair, facing the audience, with the Coach leaning in and pacing around. This is a just-before-the-game locker-room speech, the crowd audible in the background.

   Ready? Lead your crowd in roaring for a fight, bring the roar down to a soft yell, then out altogether. Signal the Coach to begin.

Script

Coach: Elijah, you heard the crowds out there, right?

Elijah: Yeah.

Coach: Well, they weren't cheering for you. You got four hundred prophets of Baal up on that mountain and there's just one of you. You know what that means?

Elijah: You're going to cheer for them?

Coach: Of course not! I'm in your corner, Elijah! Whadaya think a coach is for? But I'll tell you, it's not looking good.

Elijah: What do you think I should do?

Coach: Well, it's your decision, but if I was you I'd run away. Just get out of here and live to fight another day.

Elijah: I can't do that.

Coach: That's what I like about you, kid. You're all heart. But you're not being real bright here. Do the math. Four hundred to one. Do yourself a favor and head for the hills.

Elijah: But you don't understand. It's not just me who'll be up there. God will be with me.

Coach: Great. Now it's four hundred to two. Not a whole lot better.

Elijah: Except God is all-powerful. He can do anything. I'm not worried about those four hundred prophets. I wouldn't care if there were four thousand of them!

Coach: Then at least do this: Carry these matches with you. If you call down fire from heaven and it doesn't show up, at least you got something up your sleeve.

Elijah: Not a chance. Not only won't I cheat, I'll prove God is alive and all-powerful. I'll soak the sacrifice with water. I'll soak the wood on the altar with water. I'll even soak the altar with water!

Coach: Well, then there's nothing else I can do for you, Elijah. Go out there and we'll see what happens. Good luck, kid.

Elijah *exits,* Coach *looks up toward heaven*

Coach: I hope you take care of him, God. He's in for a tough afternoon if you don't.

Digging Deeper

~ Elijah was up against stiff odds. Why was he so confident?

~ Have you ever had to take a stand for what's right like Elijah? What happened?

~ Someone once said, "God plus me equals a majority." Do you agree or disagree? Why?

Scripture
2 Chronicles 20

Props
none

Characters
Narrator
Messenger
Jehoshaphat
Levite
Singers

Scene Setup
The story of *Jehoshaphat's* military victory is powerful and vivid, yet many children may not be familiar with this demonstration of God's power and knowledge of the future.

In this reenactment of the story, some/all of your children will play the People of Judah. You will instruct them to gather, listen to *King Jehoshaphat*, and bow down when told to do so. Then they will become the army of Judah, praising God and watching the battle. Have the children sit a few feet back from the front of the performance area, and some/all of them come forward when Jehoshaphat asks them to.

Say, "People of Judah, an army is coming against you. Your king, Jehoshaphat, is going to ask God what to do. Listen."

Script

Jehoshaphat *sits in middle of performance area,* Messenger *enters*

Messenger: O King, a vast army is coming against you. Three of our enemies have united to make war on us. They want to overthrow the kingdom!

Jehoshaphat: [*alarmed*] I must inquire of the Lord. I proclaim a fast for all Judah. I ask all my people to come together and seek help from the Lord.

People of Judah come closer. Levite *and* Singers *are with them.*

Narrator: The people of Judah came from every town and together they stood in Jerusalem, in front of the great courtyard by the temple of the Lord. The king prayed aloud.

Jehoshaphat: Lord, God of our fathers, are you not the God who is in heaven? You rule over all the kingdoms of the nations. Power and might are in your hand and no one can withstand you. Here are men coming from territories to drive us out of the land you gave us. We have no power to face this vast army that is attacking us. We do not know what to do, but our eyes are on you.

Narrator: The spirit of the Lord came on a Levite in the assembly, and he spoke.

Levite: Listen, King Jehoshaphat and all who live in Judah and Jerusalem. The Lord says not to be discouraged or afraid. For the battle is not yours, but God's. Tomorrow march down against them. Take up your positions and stand firm. See the deliverance the Lord will give you. The Lord will be with you.

Narrator: The king bowed with his face to the ground, and all the people fell down in worship before the Lord.

King Jehoshaphat *and people bow down*

Narrator: Early the next morning, they left as they had been instructed. [*people now become army gathered behind* Singers] At the head of the small army went men singing praises to the Lord.

Singers: [*speaking*] Give thanks to the Lord, for his love endures forever.

Narrator: As the Israelites sang, the Lord set ambushes against the tribes marching against Israel. The tribes began to fight among themselves, then they savagely turned on each other. [*army and* Singers *look out over audience, pointing and pretending to speak about what they see*] No one had escaped the fighting. All their enemies were dead. [*army jumps up and down, waving their hands over their heads as the victors*]

Narrator: All had come to pass exactly as the Lord had predicted.

Digging Deeper

- If you were the king, would you have marched out to face the army?

- God predicted what would happen and the king believed God. Do you believe God when, in the Bible, he promises what will happen?

- What is a promise from God that you're trusting he'll keep?

Call in Now

Scripture
Isaiah 7:14; 9:6, 7

Props
two chairs
Bibles for as many children as possible

Characters
Radio Host
Dr. Jerzy

Scene Setup
This is an especially fun skit—because some of it isn't scripted! Divide the children into four teams. Ask Team One to look up and read Isaiah 7:14. Ask Team Two to look up and read Isaiah 9:6. Ask Team Three to look up and read Isaiah 9:7. Ask Team Four to look up and read Luke 2:6, 7 and Micah 5:2.

Instruct each team to choose a spokesperson, and tell that person to respond by saying, "I know that," when it's time to make a call about what his or her team has looked up. The cue is the line, "Call in now."

Place your actors in chairs facing the audience. Ask children to sit in their teams.

Script

Radio Host: Welcome to the *What Do You Think?* radio call-in program. My guest today is one of Jerusalem's best known Pharisees, Dr. Israel Jerzy.

Dr. Jerzy: Thanks for having me. It's a great honor to be here, especially since radio and telephones won't be invented for another 1800 years or so.

Radio Host: Doctor, let's talk about your new best-seller, *Promises*. You say Jesus, who was crucified a few years ago, was actually God's Son. This can't make the other Pharisees happy.

Dr. Jerzy: You're right. But after studying Isaiah and Micah, I've decided there's just too much evidence that Jesus was holy. That Jesus was God's Son. And that He was sent to earth for us.

Radio Host: You claim Jesus' life fulfilled a number of prophesies given about the Messiah.

Dr. Jerzy: Exactly. And that's the best proof Jesus was God's Son.

Radio Host: If you're listening and know a prophesy about where God's Son was supposed to be born, call in now . . .

Takes the "call" when the Team Four spokesperson answers this challenge. She reads Luke 2:6, 7 and Micah 5:2.

Dr. Jerzy: That's right. Also, Jesus came from the family of David. There's a prophesy about that, too. Call if you know where to find that prophesy in the Bible.

Takes the "call" when the Team Three spokesperson answers this challenge. He reads Isaiah 9:7.

Radio Host: And how about a prophesy that says a boy would be born who would become the leader of his people—that the government would be on His shoulders? If you know where that prophesy can be found, call in now . . .

Takes the "call" when the Team Two spokesperson answers this challenge. She reads Isaiah 9:6.

Dr. Jerzy: Let's take one more call. How about a prophesy that says a virgin will have a child who will be called Immanuel? Call in now . . .

Takes the "call" when the Team One spokesperson answers this challenge. He reads Isaiah 7:14.

Radio Host: It appears you were right, Doctor. Many of our listeners are aware of prophesies that show Jesus is God's Son—and that he was sent to earth for us.

Dr. Jerzy: And that's what I call good news!

Radio Host: Thanks for being with us tonight, Doctor. Stay tuned for sports. The Jerusalem Jets pulled off the upset of the season by squeaking past the Samaritan Sheepherders in triple overtime. Details coming up.

Digging Deeper

ج If there were clues about who Jesus was, why didn't more people realize he was God's Son?

ج How do you think people who wrote the prophesies felt when Jesus didn't come during their lifetimes?

ج How do you feel about Jesus not yet returning for his second coming?

Missing the Point

Scripture
Luke 10:25-37

Props
chair

Characters
Jesus
Peter
Matthew
John

Scene Setup
Notify your children that this is "back to school" time; some/all of them will play the part of students during this skit. Except they're *Jesus'* students. They are disciples who are gathered around him as he teaches. Position the actor portraying *Jesus* in a chair and seat the students on the floor around him. Distribute imaginary pencils and paper to them. They will use these imaginary props to take notes as *Jesus* speaks.

—— Script ——

Jesus: Today you're going to learn about helping others and loving others as yourself. A man was going down from Jerusalem to Jericho when he fell into the hands of robbers.

Peter: Excuse me, Jesus, but how many robbers were there?

Jesus: That isn't really important to the story, Peter. Let's continue. A man was going down from Jerusalem to Jericho when—

John: Jesus, will the going-to-Jericho part be on the test?

Jesus: Where the man was going isn't as important as what happens in the story, John.

John: Okay, just checking. Thanks.

Jesus: A man was going down from Jerusalem to Jericho when he fell into the hands of robbers. They stripped him of his clothes, beat him, and . . . yes, Peter?

Peter: How many "p's" in "stripped?"

Matthew: Two "p's," Pete.

Peter: You sure?

Matthew: Absolutely. Otherwise it's "striped," like my robe. And robbers don't jump out from behind rocks to *stripe* a guy's clothes.

Jesus: Gentlemen! You're missing the point. We're talking about how to help and love our neighbors. This is important!

John: That's why we don't want to miss anything, Jesus. This is important stuff to know.

Jesus: Yes, it is important to know. But I don't want you to just know about helping others, I want you to do it. Don't just listen with your heads—listen with your hearts, too.

Matthew: Sorry we've been interrupting, Jesus.

Jesus: You're forgiven. Are you ready to listen for the truth in this parable now?

Peter: One more thing: are you going to serve snacks at the end of the lesson?

Digging Deeper

 ﹖ Why is it important to know the teachings of Jesus? Why is it important to follow them? Which is more difficult for you? Why?

 ﹖ Why do you think Jesus used parable stories to teach? Did it work?

Food or Fertilizer?

Scripture
Mark 6:30-44

Props
fish-shaped snack crackers (optional)

Characters
Jerry
Daniel

Scene Setup
Have some/all of the children be guests at the most famous impromptu picnic of all time: the one at which Jesus fed over 5,000 people with five loaves and two fish! If you want to serve a snack today, consider fish-shaped crackers.

Tell the picnic guests the story found in Mark 6:30-44. Stress that the crowd of at least 5,000 was in the wilderness. No food was available. The crowd was hungry and willing to pay anything for a meal. At least, that's what Jerry is counting on! Jerry is positioned on one side of the performance area and Daniel is in the middle of it. Tell the children to mill around patting their stomachs as if they've just finished huge meals.

— Script —

Jerry *enters, pretending to push a heavily-loaded cart. He addresses* Daniel.

Jerry: Whew! I thought I'd never get here!

Daniel: That's quite a load you've got in the cart there.

Jerry: Yep—three hundred pounds of fried fish and enough buns to make fish sandwiches for every man, woman, and child in this crowd.

Daniel: And you wheeled it all the way out here?

Jerry: Every inch, buddy. Up hills, across ravines, under the blazing sun. It about killed me.

Daniel: But why? Why haul all this food out here?

Jerry: When I heard you all tromped out here without bringing lunch, I knew this was my chance to get rich. I took every penny I had, bought all this food, and now I'm in the sandwich business. [*calling to the crowd*] Step right up, folks. Jerry's Lunch Stand is now open!

Daniel: Ummm, Jerry, there's something you should know.

Jerry: [*continuing to call*] The line forms on the right. Don't be shy! Step right over. [*to Daniel*] So what's the deal? How come nobody is moving?

Daniel: Maybe it's because they're so stuffed from eating.

Jerry: Eating? Are you nuts? What's there to eat out here? Dirt?

Daniel: Well, Jesus took five loaves and two fish and he fed everyone.

Jerry: With five loaves and two fish?! That's not possible!

Daniel: I know. It was a miracle.

Jerry: What'd he charge for the food? He must have made a killing!

Daniel: He didn't charge anything. It was free.

Jerry: So now what? What do I do with all this fish?

Daniel: I don't know. But I'd appreciate if you'd move it downwind. It's been out in the sun a long time and it's starting to smell.

Jerry: This is going to ruin me. I'm sunk! Unless . . . [*calling to the crowd*] Step right up, ladies and gentlemen! Fertilizer for sale! Fresh fertilizer for sale!

Digging Deeper

- How was it possible for Jesus to do things no one else could do?

- What are other miracles Jesus performed?

- If you could have seen Jesus perform a miracle, would it make your faith in Jesus stronger? Why or why not?

We Will Not Bow Down

Scripture
Daniel 3

Props
none

Characters
Narrator
Group One (three to five children)
Group Two (three to five children)
Group Three (the remaining children)

Scene Setup
This skit is a Readers Theater, which means the children will read the script aloud together. Explain that the script is based on Daniel, chapter 3. This is the story of three young men who would not compromise their faith in God—even if it cost them their lives. Rehearse *Group Three's* line several times.

Once the children have mastered this script, consider sharing their reading of it with an adult class, or during the morning worship service.

Note: This skit doesn't finish the story—you can do that in your group or let this skit whet children's appetite to read the entire story in the book of Daniel.

Script

Narrator:	It came to pass that King Nebuchadnezzar ordered his workmen to create a statue ninety feet high and nine feet wide. Goldsmiths hammered gold into gleaming sheets and fixed the rich metal to the statue. The gilded image shone above the plain of Dura in the province of Babylon.
Group One:	Then the king summoned governors, judges, and other officials.
Group Two:	This is what you are commanded to do. When you hear the sound of the king's royal band, you must bow down and worship the image of gold.
Group Three:	We will not bow down.
Group Two:	Those who do not bow down will be thrown into a blazing furnace and burned alive.
Group Three:	We will not bow down.

Group One: Men came forward and told the king that not everyone was obeying the royal law.

Group Two: King, may you live forever! You have given orders that when your royal music sounds, all must bow down.

Group Three: We will not bow down.

Group Two: But three men refuse to bow down to the god you have made.

Narrator: The king was furious. He called for Shadrach, Meshach, and Abednego, who were brought before the him.

Group One: You have refused to bow down. You will have one more chance. Bow or be burned alive.

Group Three: We will not bow down. Throw us into a burning furnace and our God will save us. Even if he does not save us, we will not serve your god.

Narrator: Shadrach, Meshach, and Abednego were shackled and taken to a blazing furnace. There they were thrown in.

Group One: We will not bow down.

Group Two: We will not bow down.

Group Three: We will not bow down.

All Groups: We will not bow down.

Digging Deeper

- If you had been Shadrach, Meshach, and Abednego, would you have been scared to stand up to the king?
- Shadrach, Meshach, and Abednego served only the one true God. Do you serve just that one God? How?
- What happened to Shadrach, Meshach, and Abednego? How did the king respond? You can find the answers in Daniel 3.

Who's Got the Body?

Scripture
Mark 16

Props
none

Characters
Peter
Roman Captain
Samuel the Pharisee
Moderator

Scene Setup
Ask the audience to be the jury who will decide which of the three characters is telling the truth. That means they must pay careful attention—they'll be voting when the investigation is over. The "witnesses" stand in front of the performance area.

Script

Peter, *the* Roman Captain, Pharisee Samuel, *and the* Moderator *stand in front*

Moderator: Everyone knows what happened recently in Jerusalem. Jesus was arrested, tried, and then killed. After being crucified, his body was sealed in a tomb. A large stone was rolled in front of the entrance. But Jesus' body has disappeared, and the jury wants to know what happened to it. Please state your names and tell what you think happened.

Roman Captain: I am a Captain in the Imperial Roman Army. My men were guarding the tomb so no one could steal the body. I'm not sure what happened, but my men were overpowered by something not of this world.

Moderator: What do you mean?

Roman Captain: Just what I said. My men aren't afraid of anything. But something scared them half to death. An angel or a ghost, I don't know what it was. But I'll tell you one thing: We Romans don't have Jesus' body. If we did, we'd haul it out to quiet all the rumors going around.

Samuel: Well, we certainly don't have Jesus' body—but I think I know who does have it. I am Samuel, a Pharisee. I think Jesus' disciples stole his body so they could tell their ridiculous story about Jesus' coming back to life.

Roman Captain: Are you saying some fishermen and tax collectors overpowered my soldiers and moved that stone? No way!

Samuel: Then you explain what happened!

Roman Captain: I don't know what happened! But whoever has that body is in big trouble.

Peter: I can tell you what happened to Jesus' body.

Moderator: And your name?

Peter: Peter. I'm a follower of Jesus. And I know why his body wasn't in the tomb. Jesus came back to life.

Samuel: Impossible!

Peter: Well, you Pharisees don't have it or you'd show it to stop the talking. You Romans don't have it or you'd do the same thing. And we didn't take it. We were scared when Jesus was crucified, and we hid. That leaves the obvious answer: Jesus really did rise from the dead.

Roman Captain: He's got a point . . .

Samuel: Are you crazy? Simply impossible.

Roman Captain: Then you explain it.

Moderator: Let's have the jury decide. Raise your hands if you believe the Romans have Jesus' body. Raise your hands if you believe the Pharisees have it. Raise your hands if you think the disciples stole it. Now raise your hands if you believe Jesus rose from the dead just like he promised he'd do. Looks like that settles it—jury dismissed!

Digging Deeper

- What were the disciples afraid of when Jesus was crucified? Did that change? What happened?

- If Jesus came back to life after dying, that makes him our Savior. Do you think of Jesus as your Savior? Why or why not?

- With whom have you shared this Good News? Name a person you could share it with this week.

Jailhouse Rock

Scripture
Acts 16:16-34

Props
none

Characters
Paul
Silas
Jailer
Prisoner One
Prisoner Two
Narrator

Scene Setup
Have some/all of the children be prisoners locked in a Roman jail with *Paul* and *Silas*. There are no windows, no regular meals, and the entire jail smells like a very old, very unwashed gym sock. Instruct prisoners to listen and act according to the instructions they'll hear. Arrange children around *Paul* and *Silas*, who sit together in the center of the performance area. Place the *Jailer* to one side, ready for a dramatic entrance. Place *Prisoner One* and *Prisoner Two* in the jail.

——— Script ———

Narrator:	After Paul and Silas were arrested for healing a slave girl, they were beaten and flogged. Then they were thrown into prison and placed in the inner cell with their feet in stocks. They were bruised and bleeding, yet even at midnight they continued to sing and praise God.
Paul and Silas:	[*singing*] Jesus loves me this I know.
Prisoner One:	Will you two be quiet?
Prisoner Two:	It's midnight! The rest of us are trying to get some sleep!
Paul:	But when we know Jesus loves us, how can we be silent?
Silas:	We want to praise God!

Prisoner One: Look, if Jesus loves you so much, why are you sitting in this jail?

Prisoner Two: With your feet locked in stocks, no less. Seems to me like your Jesus has forgotten all about you.

Paul: Jesus is our Savior—now and forever!

Prisoner Two: Yeah, right.

Narrator: Suddenly, there was a violent earthquake that shook the prison's very foundation. The prisoners fell to the left . . . then to the right . . . then they fell to the floor and lay still. The jailer woke up. He ran over to the prison and saw the broken doors hanging open. He knew that if his prisoners escaped he would be killed, so he panicked. Then he heard something.

Paul: Don't harm yourself! We're all here!

Narrator: The jailer rushed in and fell down before Paul and Silas. As the other prisoners dusted themselves off, the jailer took Paul and Silas out of the jail and asked them a question.

Jailer: What must I do to be saved?

Narrator: Paul and Silas answered the jailer's question, and that night his entire family was filled with joy because they came to believe in God.

Digging Deeper

∂ If you'd been another prisoner in jail with Paul and Silas, what would you have thought of them before the earthquake? After the earthquake? Why?

∂ Do you think of Jesus as your own Savior? Why? What is Jesus saving you from?

All Sheep Go to Heaven

Scripture
Matthew 25:31-40

Props
none

Characters
Jesus
Head Sheep
Head Goat

Scene Setup
Seat some/all of the children in a group on the floor. Ask children whose birthdays occur in January, February, March, April, May, and June to raise their hands. Tell these children they will be one group—the "Sheep." Tell children whose birthdays occur in other months that they'll be "Goats."

Script

Jesus faces the group; Head Sheep *is in the middle of the Sheep and* Head Goat *is in the middle of the Goats*

Jesus: This is Judgment Day and I am Jesus. I will now form you into two groups. To my right, I want all the sheep to gather. If you are a sheep, please go there now.

Pauses while Sheep move

Jesus: The rest of you are goats. Please go to my left.

Pauses while Goats move

Jesus: Sheep, you will go to heaven with me. Goats, [*pause*] you won't go to heaven.

Head Goat: What gives? We loved and served you!

Jesus: I was hungry and you didn't give me food. I was naked and you didn't clothe me. I was sick and in prison and you didn't visit me.

Head Goat: But when did we have a chance? We were never with you until now!

Jesus: Sure you were with me. Not with me, exactly, but with people who needed you.

Head Sheep: Umm, Lord, I think you've made a slight mistake with us, too.

Jesus: What mistake would that be?

Head Sheep: It's not that we're not grateful. We want to go to heaven, but we've talked it over and, well, none of us ever gave you a meal. Or even a worn-out coat. We never visited you in prison or when you were sick.

Jesus: But what you did for even the least of my brothers you did for me. There's been no mistake made here.

Head Goat: Jesus? We were just wondering something.

Jesus: Yes?

Head Goat: If we'd known that it was important to you how we treated needy people, we'd have been better about it. Really. We'd have been generous. Caring. We'd have helped out.

Jesus: But I told you about caring for others. Why didn't you listen?

Head Goat: Okay, we were wrong. We admit that. But now that you've reminded us, we'll do better. Like, maybe you need lunch right now. Or a new pair of sandals. We'll take up an offering and buy them for you.

Jesus: Sorry. The time for second chances is over. It's time for the sheep to come into life that lasts forever and for the goats to enter into punishment that will never end.

Digging Deeper

- If Judgment Day were today, would you be a sheep or a goat? Why?
- What can you do to treat needy people like you'd treat Jesus?
- If Jesus cares so much about the poor and sick, why doesn't he just give them what they need?

Scripture
Exodus 20

Props
pencil
paper
chair

Characters
Moses
Israelite

Scene Setup
Tell the audience that they'll act as Instant Judges, voting "innocent" by pointing thumbs up and "guilty" by pointing thumbs down. Ask the children to practice their signals several times before starting the skit.

Script

Israelite *sits in chair, pretending to hold the reins of a donkey pulling a cart. Moses enters from stage left.*

Moses: Hold up there!

Israelite: [*to donkey*] Whoa, Nellie. [*to Moses*] Yes, can I help you?

Moses: I'd like to talk with you about—

Israelite: Hey—you're Moses, right? The guy who's leading this exodus from Egypt?

Moses: Yes, but—

Israelite: Wait'll I tell them back home that I met you! They're not going to believe it!

Moses: Actually, I was hoping to talk with you about—

Israelite: What are you doing pulling over donkey carts? I mean, was I speeding or something?

Moses: I want to talk to you about the Ten Commandments.

Israelite: Yeah, I heard you read them when you came down from Mt. Sinai. Great stuff.

Moses: But are you keeping the Ten Commandments?

Israelite: You mean obeying them?

Moses: Yes, that's why I pulled you over. This is a routine check to see if you're obeying the Commandments. If you're not, I'll have to write you a ticket. [*holds up pencil and paper as if it's a ticket book*] First, no other gods before the true God?

Israelite: Absolutely!

Moses: You've never skipped gathering to praise God to go do something else?

Israelite: Well, once or twice a few of us snuck away to go fishing—which is hard to do when you're crossing a wilderness.

Moses: And when did you do this? On the Sabbath?

Israelite: Sure—when else do we have a day off?

Moses: So you have broken the Commandments, Commandment Number Four—keeping the Sabbath day holy—and that would also be breaking Commandment Number One—putting no other gods before the true God.

Israelite Hey! Going fishing isn't a god!

Moses: Anything that's more important than knowing and worshiping God is an idol. Sorry.

Israelite: Can I talk to someone else about this? I don't think you're being fair!

Moses: Let's ask some judges. How many of you think this Israelite is breaking the Commandment about keeping the Sabbath day holy? Thumbs up if innocent and thumbs down if guilty. [*pauses for audience vote*] And how about placing something before God? Guilty or innocent? [*pauses for audience vote*]

Israelite: [*to audience*] Look, I take back what I told Moses. Let's pretend it never happened. He didn't hear me right because he wasn't listening!

Moses: [*writing in notepad*] Commandment Number Nine: False testimony against a neighbor.

Israelite: I'm going to grab that ticket and tear it up—that's what I'll do!

Moses: [*writing in notepad*] Stealing. Boy, this just gets worse and worse.

Israelite: Look, Moses, so I'm not perfect. But these Commandments are so hard!

Moses: You're right, the Ten Commandments are hard to keep. They show us what God is like. He's holy. So far I haven't found anyone who's kept them all perfectly, including me.

Israelite: Then what can I do?

Moses: Do what I do: Go to God for forgiveness. He's holy, but he's also loving.

Israelite: Thanks for the advice. I'll just be going now.

Moses: Sorry, but I do have to give you one ticket. [*hands paper to Israelite*] This is a No Parking Zone. Have a nice day.

Moses walks away

Digging Deeper

≈ Has anyone ever kept all of the Ten Commandments? Who? Give reasons to support your answer.

≈ Can obeying rules make you holy and perfect before God? Why or why not?

≈ If obeying rules can't make us holy, what or who can? How?

Fruit Tree Wannabe

Scripture
Galatians 5:22, 23

Props
banana
apple
orange
pinecone
tape or twine

Characters
Tree One
Tree Two

Scene Setup
Have some/all of the children be an orchard of fruit trees. *Tree One* is kind and caring. *Tree Two* is defensive and angry. Hang an apple on *Tree One* with twine or tape. Hang an apple, orange, banana, and pinecone on *Tree Two*. Instruct the rest of the children to stand, positioning themselves with about three feet between them. They'll raise their arms, and you don't want any mid-air collisions!

Ask children to individually decide if they're apple trees, pear trees, or orange trees, but to not tell anyone what they've chosen to be. Ask children to assume a "tree position" with raised arms. After they've demonstrated their abilities, ask them to drop their arms and only assume their tree positions when they're asked to later.

Script

Tree One: So, how you doing?

Tree Two: Okay.

Tree One: After that frost last night, I figured I'd lose some leaves—but I think I'm okay.

Tree Two: [*sarcastically*] Good for you.

Tree One: Say, you've got quite a collection of fruit there.

Tree Two: Yeah, I've got a great crop, huh.

Tree One: And I don't remember you being there yesterday.

Tree Two: [*defensively*] I just moved into the orchard. Why? You got a problem with that?

Tree One: Well, the rest of us were planted by the gardener years ago, and he didn't plant you. I don't understand how you got here.

Tree Two: Look, I planted myself, all right? I snuck in here last night and planted myself. And I grew all this fruit last night, too.

Tree One: But you can't grow fruit. You're a pine tree. You just grow pinecones.

Tree Two: [*angrily*] You can see the fruit with your own eyes, buddy. I'm a pinecone-apple-orange-banana tree.

Tree One: You can't be. See out there in the orchard? Those are banana trees.[*banana trees assume tree position*] And those are orange trees. [*orange trees assume tree position*] And those are apple trees, like me. [*apple trees assume tree position*]

Tree Two: What's your point?

Tree One: My point is that the gardener carefully planted and pruned us so we can bear fruit. You can't just decide to grow fruit. Besides, your fruit is taped on.

Tree Two: Well, I decided to be a fruit tree. So I joined an orchard and I stuck on some fruit. That makes me a fruit tree.

Tree One: Except we keep producing fruit, and yours is going to rot and fall off.

Tree Two: [*sarcastically*] You're just full of good news, aren't you? I'll bet you get invited to lots of parties.

Tree One: Look, let's talk to the gardener about it. He can make fruit grow on some of the least-likely plants.

Tree Two: [*hopefully*] You think he could help me grow fruit?

Tree One: He's the only gardener who could. We can give it a try.

Tree Two: Great! Thanks! And by the way, I'm getting hungry. How about giving me an apple? [*tries to grab* Tree One's *apple*]

Tree One: Hey!

Tree Two: Oh, sorry.

Digging Deeper

ʒ Think about a grown-up in your church you respect. What fruit of the Spirit do you see in that person? How do you see it shown?

ʒ Of the fruits of the spirit listed in Galatians 5:22 and 23, which do you see in yourself?

Worship Resources

Each of the skits in this book correlates to a unit of worship from Standard Publishing's two-year series of Worship Folders for elementary kids. The worship series was developed to help children worship God for who he is and what he has done. Each eight-page folder is a thematic unit with Scripture activities, music, prayer suggestions, and small group ideas for four sessions of children's worship.

Listed with each skit title below is the correlating Worship Folder and its order number.

Way Back in Time
God Is Creator (42241)

Sunny With 100% Chance of Rain
God Is a Promise Keeper (42247)

Celestial Drive-Thru Up Ahead
God Is Our Caregiver (42248)

Last One There Gets the Lobby
Jesus Is Immanuel (42251)

Seeing by Believing
Jesus Is God's Son (42252)

Up a Tree
Jesus Is Our Friend (42246)

Live at the Jordan River
God Is Forgiving (42243)

An Eye-Opening Experience
Jesus Is Alive (42255)

Knee-Deep in Sheep
Jesus Is Our Shepherd (42249)

The Position Has Been Filled
God Is Sovereign (42250)

From Everlasting to Everlasting
God Is Eternal (42244)

No Time to Wait
Jesus Is Our Hope (42256)

Giant Trouble
God Is Ever-Present (42245)

Against All Odds
God Is Powerful (42242)

What War?
God Is All-Knowing (42254)

Call in Now
Jesus Is Messiah (42257)

Missing the Point
Jesus Is Our Teacher (42258)

Food or Fertilizer?
Jesus, Miracle Doer (42259)

We Will Not Bow Down
God, the Only God (42260)

Who's Got the Body?
Jesus Is Good News (42261)

Jailhouse Rock
Jesus Is Savior (42253)

All Sheep Go to Heaven
Jesus Is Love (42262)

Commandment Cop
God Is Holy (42263)

Fruit Tree Wannabe
God Is Inside Us (42264)